30 Students in 30 Days & Repeat

A 30-day Marketing Challenge to Grow
Your Dance, Gymnastics, Martial Arts, or Music Business

By Gina Evans

Grace and Gwendolyn, may you live a debt free life.

30 Students in 30 Days & Repeat

A 30-day Marketing Challenge to Grow
Your Dance, Gymnastics, Martial Arts, or Music Business

Introduction	Page 9
Challenge Day 1 Business Cards	Page 12
Challenge Day 2 Social Media	Page 17
Challenge Day 3 YouTube	Page 22
Challenge Day 4 Website	Page 27
Challenge Day 5 Pay-per-click Ads	Page 34
Challenge Day 6 Email Blast	Page 39
Challenge Day 7 Know Your Competition	Page 44

Challenge Day 8   Page 48
    Identify Your Unique Selling Points

Challenge Day 9   Page 53
    Door Hangers

Challenge Day 10   Page 58
    Press Releases

Challenge Day 11   Page 61
    Referrals

Challenge Day 12   Page 66
    Answer the Phone/Office Hours

Challenge Day 13   Page 71
    Letters to Teachers at Schools

Challenge Day 14   Page 74
    Sell to Current Students

Challenge Day 15   Page 78
    Call Past Students

Challenge Day 16   Page 82
    Free Clinics/Free Trial Class

Challenge Day 17　　　　　　　　　　Page 86
　　　Many Uses of Postcards

Challenge Day 18　　　　　　　　　　Page 89
　　　Community Outreach

Challenge Day 19　　　　　　　　　　Page 93
　　　Meetups/Deal Sites

Challenge Day 20　　　　　　　　　　Page 97
　　　Testimonials

Challenge Day 21　　　　　　　　　　Page 100
　　　Direct Mail

Challenge Day 22　　　　　　　　　　Page 104
　　　Banners/Signs/Yard Signs

Challenge Day 23　　　　　　　　　　Page 108
　　　Person-to-Person Marketing

Challenge Day 24　　　　　　　　　　Page 112
　　　T-shirts/Bumper Stickers

Challenge Day 25　　　　　　　　　　Page 115
　　　Online Reviews

Challenge Day 26   Page 119
     Chamber of Commerce/Networking Groups

Challenge Day 27   Page 123
     Blog

Challenge Day 28   Page 126
     Promote with Other Businesses

Challenge Day 29   Page 129
     Information in Windows/Fliers Outside

Challenge Day 30   Page 132
     CLEAN!

Repeat   Page 136

Introduction

30 Students in 30 Days & Repeat is a 30-day marketing challenge to grow your studio, school, or gym. No matter what age you teach, or whether it's dance, gymnastics, music, martial arts, or anything, really, this challenge will work for you. We all want that one idea that will bring 30, 50, or even a 100 students, but have you found it yet?

With *30 Students in 30 Days & Repeat*, you will have a daily marketing challenge to help you gain one student per day. Yes, some ideas may get you more than one and another idea may result in a new student down the road, but by the end of your 30 days you will have the potential to have 30 or more new students. Then you repeat the process. Just think, you could have 90 students in 3 months.

To start you need to know your numbers…exactly. "I have about 100 students," does not cut it! Knowing your exact number is the only way you will know if your marketing is working. Before you start the 30-day challenge, I want you to figure out exactly how many students you have. Take that number and write it nice and big on the page to your right.

You need to start actively tracking which marketing ideas gain new students. It can be as simple as tally marks on a piece of paper at your desk. By tracking which students come from which marketing idea you will know where to put your energy and money in the future.

For example: Idea A brings you zero students, it is free, and it takes up a huge chunk of your time while idea B brought you 4 new students, cost you $2,000, and took very little of your time. Which one would you repeat? If you are not tracking which marketing idea brings in which students you would not know which one is the better choice for you. Now let us get started on the 30-day marketing challenge!

Day 1 Challenge - Business Cards

Business cards are one of your top marketing pieces. They are very low cost and you can get them quickly. My favorite site for any print material is gotprint.com. They have great prices, a lot of products and are easy to use. At the time of writing this, you can get 500 full color, front-and-back printed, standard size business cards for under $15. There is so much you can do with business cards, which is why it is the first challenge of this book.

Ok, you are reading this thinking, "I have business cards...somewhere." Well I say throw them out, if you can find them, and let us start over together. Business cards are no longer just filler for your Rolodex or only meant to make your desk look official; they are 100% a marketing tool, and you need to think of them that way.

Your business cards should have your business name and what you do, address, phone number, email, and website as well as a

13

full color photo on the front (remember, a picture is worth a thousand words, and your name might not be obvious to everyone). On the back, print FREE TRIAL CLASS with a "call to action"–"Call Now," "Sign Up Now," and "Start Today"–are a few of my favorites. Without a call to action, your business card will not get acted on. You need to tell people what you want them to do.

You do not need to have one consistent business card style for your business. Create a few different business cards featuring different ages or classes on each card. For example, for a dance studio, have one card showing 3 year-olds dancing, another with teens doing cheerleading, and a third featuring your adult classes. This way you can be more direct with your person-to-person marketing (more on this on Challenge Day 23).

When you hand out your business card to anyone, always give two. Ask them to pass on the second one to someone they know who might be interested in your business. Word of mouth is the best advertising, but you have to remember to ask for it. Also, leave your business cards EVERYWHERE. Go out to eat and leave them on the table with your tip; at a hotel in your area, leave them in the room or in the common areas; while grabbing a coffee, leave a few inside the shop.

Anytime you're at the library, post office, doctor's office, or anywhere you go to sit or stand and wait for something, leave a few business cards. Someone will be in your same spot waiting in the future. Yes, the cards might get thrown away, but they might get picked up and lead to a new student.

Print business cards for each of your teachers with their names on them. Tell them about the same thing you just read. Start a competition that whichever teacher has the most students bring in his or her business cards and tries a free trial class in the next two months gets a prize. The prize can be anything, but most teachers love a gift card. Considering the average student stays two years, pays $50 a month, and takes 20 months of classes (to make math easy), that one student has brought you $1000. Say you order four sets of business cards for $60 and give out one $25 gift card to the teacher who won your competition. You have just spent $85 to earn $1000–not a bad return on your investment.

Day 1 Challenge - Update and Actively Use Your Business Cards

- Design 3 styles of cards with a clear "call to action" and free trial class information
- Order cards for each of your teachers
- Sit with your teachers and explain the purpose of their business cards and the new student competition
- Leave your business cards everywhere and hand two cards to anyone you meet
- Make it your goal to successfully and actively go through 500 cards during this 30-day challenge

Day 2 Challenge - Social Media

Social Media is an active, ever-changing world of advertising opportunities. I know that even as I write this, new sites will appear, others will disappear, and many platforms will change their rules. Basically, you need to stay relevant in the online market. If you are already getting anxious and your hands are sweating from the thought of today's challenge, do not put this book down! You can do this—remember you do not have to do it by yourself. Find a teen in your business, a young 20-something family member, or even a college student to help you.

Currently, the big social media sites out there are Facebook, Twitter, SnapChat, Instagram, Linkedin, and YouTube. YouTube is such a huge part of all of these that it will get its own challenge day. Today we are going to focus on the others. I am going to go forward assuming either you are familiar with these sites or you have enlisted the help of someone who is.

Step one: If you do not have a business page on each of these sites, start there. Each of these sites has a different feel and following, but 90% of your content can be shared on all of them. You may want to look into a website that can link all of your social media sites together and allow you to schedule your post from one central location.

Hootesuite is what I use, but there are others out there. Note–This is not something you need to pay for; free is our friend.

Next you need to build up a base of people who like or follow your page. Go to each page and see how many followers you have. Set a goal to increase that in the next month by 10%, 15%, or 20%. Write out this goal and place it near your computer so you can see it! To increase your followers you need to invite people to your page. You need to make sure all your printed materials have the social media icons on them. That way people know you are present on all of those sites. Send out emails asking people to follow you, and then tell your Facebook followers to follow you on all your other pages. If you have social media pages but no one is looking at them or sharing the content, they are doing you about as much good as your old business cards that were sitting on your desk. Make sure all of your information on your page is correct–website, phone number, address, descriptions, etc. You do not want to have this great, free, marketing tool with an incorrect phone number.

Now you need content to post. A lot of this can be done in one day and scheduled for a month, 6 months, or even a year. Then as exciting events happen you can post them immediately, but you will have a continual presence without having to post every day. What to post? I will post an inspirational quote every day, then share a blog post or story related to my field two or three times a week. I love photos, so I post as many as I can find. I post a message or greeting for every holiday during the year, and I love to find a few crazy days like national hula hooping day or national world wish day and post about those. I will post upcoming events or news for the business. These are all things you can do one day a month. I do post most of the same items to all of the pages, but I might change the wording or a photo according to which site I am on. That way it keeps the pages fresh and different.

Social media groups are also a great addition to this marketing area. Joining and actively participating in different groups will help you promote your business. You want to make yourself the go-to person on information related to your business without selling constantly. Just offer friendly advice. As you build this image, people will start coming to you as the expert.

Day 2 Challenge - Create and Maintain Your Social Media Presence

- Create and update a page on all the major social media sites
- Increase your followers by _____% (you pick your goal)
- Schedule a month (or more) of posts to all the sites
- Throughout the month, add in new posts of significance
- Look for social media groups you can join

Day 3 Challenge - YouTube

Today's challenge is all about the power of video. If you do not already have one, it is time to start a YouTube channel for your business. YouTube started in 2005 and now has 4 billion hours worth of video each month, and people are uploading 72 hours worth of video every minute. Just like I said in yesterday's challenge, if you are already getting anxious and your hands are sweating from the thought of today's challenge—you can do this. Remember, you do not have to do it by yourself. Find someone to help you. Note—YouTube even has videos on how to start your own YouTube channel.

Once you have your channel set up, it is time to start posting videos. You need to remember that like so much of social media marketing, this is a grassroots effort. You do not need to start out with 100 videos and a thousand views. Even YouTube itself started with one video.

Now the question is what do I film a video of. Let us brainstorm together.

- Videos of valuable tips to show off your expertise in your field
- Answer specific questions customers have had (we all get those same questions over and over again)

- Conduct an interview with an expert and/or all of your employees
- Conduct an interview with students—Maybe you have a student of the month program, a student who has received scholarships or awards, or one who has done something really interesting related to your business
- Post video testimonials from your best customers (more about this on Challenge Day 20)
- Show the results of someone using your services—in short, film a class or two
- Take viewers on a tour of your business
- Create "how to" videos—As a dance and gymnastics teacher, my favorite one is how to make a hair bun! That way when parents say they cannot do their children's hair, I am able to send them to this video.
- Any performance or demonstration by you, your staff, or your students

And there are so many more… What can you come up with?

Here are a few FAQs about videos:

How long should it be?

It should be as long as is needed to get your point across, but with that in mind, note that Wistia reported that for a video of 4-5 minutes, fewer than 60% of your viewers would still be with you by the end, but 75% would still be watching by the end of a 1-2 minute video.

How do I film it?

The video does not have to be professionally filmed. As you get into making more complex videos, you might want to invest in a camera, but do not bother to run out and buy one today. Start with your smartphone. I do suggest a tripod or a DIY tripod to keep your phone steady, though. Also you can do fairly simple edits on your phone with some free apps. A few I like are: Cute Cut, Magisto, and Viddy.

How many do I have to do?

No magic number here, but just like the other social media sites, you want to keep your YouTube channel active. I would film four or five today, then you can post them and share them throughout the month.

Share them...who, how, when?

YouTube is not just for your videos to sit out there and hope someone watches them. You need to share them. Post them on your website, send them out in an email blast, and put them up on other social media sites.

Day 3 Challenge - Create Videos and Post Them to Your YouTube Channel

- o Set up a YouTube channel for your business
- o Brainstorm video ideas
- o Film four or five different videos today and upload them to YouTube
- o Share the videos throughout the month using emails and social media
- o Continue to make one (or more) videos a week

Day 4 Challenge - Website

By now everyone understands the importance of a website. Websites create credibility for your business. Websites are always accessible, which means your website is selling for you even when you are not. Honestly, not having a website means you are losing business, so if by a small chance you do not have a website, I am telling you to GET ONE TODAY! Every website should have, at the bare minimum, these five pages: home, contact us, about us, FAQs (frequently asked questions), and class information.

The problem with most small businesses is that they had a website created when they opened, then they never changed it. You cannot create a website once and walk away. The content on your website needs to change regularly. Think of websites as that one employee who works for very little money, but never stops working. Your website attracts new customers, sells to them, informs current customers, and creates credibility for your business. Today you are going to do a website assessment and overhaul.

Open up your website and honestly answer the following questions:

1. When was my website last updated?

2. Is all the information current—classes, calendar, prices, staff, location, etc.?

3. Does every page have a link back to the home page?
Are social media links on every page, or at least the main pages?

4. Are any pages too long and should either be shortened or made into two pages?

5. Is there a "call to action" on every page?

6. Am I using active and not passive voice in my text?

7. Do I have photos and are they current?

8. When I use search engines (Google, Yahoo, Bing, etc.) to find information on classes like those my business offers, does my business come up on the first page of search results?

9. Do I have a mobile site?

10. How can I make the website better?

Then, have someone who is not closely involved with your business answer the following questions:

1. Do my website pages load quickly?
2. Can you easily find my contact information?
3. Can you easily find my office hours?
4. Does my site appear to fit the "feel" of my business, and is it a pleasant online experience?
5. Are all features working on my site?
6. Are there any broken links?
7. Did it work well with your computer and browser?
8. Is it well written and easy to understand?
9. Does it answer any questions you may have about my business?
10. How can I make it better?

Now that you have done an assessment, let us fix the problems. Whether you do it yourself or you have someone else do it, spending time with your website is important. There are a few website mistakes that a lot of small businesses make. The first is having a dark background with white text. This is hard to read, no matter how cool you think it looks, so please don't do it. The second is using the wrong fonts. Fonts can set the tone of your business. Make sure they are clean, easy to read fonts. Even if the font you use for your business name is a script font, do not write your entire website with it.

The questions asked are fairly self-explanatory, so if you or your friend answered no to any of them, change it. Let us discuss some of the questions that you may be wondering if they are really a big deal.

Does every page have a link back to the home page? This may seem odd, but you want anyone to be able to go back to the home page with just one click. You may have a customer send a link to a page onto a friend. How is that person supposed to get to the home page to learn about your business?

Are any pages too long and should either be shortened or made into two pages? Do not make people scroll down to keep reading. Make the text short and to the point, and make each topic have its own page.

Do I have photos and are they current? Stock photos can make your page look unapproachable, and outdated photos will come across as your business being outdated. Additionally, poor amateur photos obviously leave a bad impression on visitors. Pictures are worth a thousand words, so make sure they are saying the right things about your business.

When I use search engines (Google, Yahoo, Bing, etc.) to find information on classes like those my business offers, does my business come up on the first page of search results? If not, then you need to make sure your page titles, descriptions, and keywords are active on every page and are logical words that people would use to search for your site. If you do not know what I am talking about, Google it.

Does my site appear to fit the "feel" of my business, and is it a pleasant online experience? This is a big one; you do not want to push away potential clients because your website was not a pleasant experience. You also do not want to entice the wrong customers. Make sure your website is speaking to the type of students you want.

This website is your 24-hour selling tool, so make sure it is up to date and reaching all of the right people. Even the best websites out there could use a little makeover. Do not assume that just because you love your site, everyone else does, too.

Day 4 Challenge – Website Assessment and Makeover

- Take the 10 question assessment
- Have someone else take the other 10 question assessment
- Review your answers and start making changes

Day 5 Challenge - Pay-per-click Ads

Facebook, LinkedIn, Bing, and Google all have pay-per-click advertising (PPC). If you are not familiar with it these are the ads that appear on the page either at the top or off to the side. Each of the four sites has their own requirements and specifications, but they are all basically the same concept. You create an ad and set a daily, weekly, or monthly budget. When they click on the ad they are taken to your website. You pay according to the number of impressions your ad makes (the amount of times it is seen) and the number of times people click on the ad. The system does not go over your monthly budget. These are great marketing tools to drive traffic to your website. When you create your ad, you get a headline and a short description. Only so many characters are allowed, so you'll have to keep it short. The headline needs to be your call to action, NOT your business name, and the description needs to be a short sentence to get them to click the ad. Here is a great example of a Google Adwords for a dance studio:

Sign up for Dance Class Now

Jazz and tap classes all levels and ages now open

It is short and to the point. Plus, it makes you want to click the link to learn more.

With Google Adwords and Bing, you will be asked for keywords when making your ad. This is how your ad knows when to appear. You need to include classes you teach, your location, cities near you, and pretty much any word you think someone will put into a search engine to look for what you have to offer. I also always put in the names of my competitors; that way, if someone is looking for them by name, my ad will appear. There is a negative keyword option – this allows you to pick keywords used in searches you do not want to appear on. For example, if you are a music school that only teaches string instruments, you might want to put wood and percussion instruments in your negative keywords.

Facebook and LinkedIn will ask for demographic information so they can place your ads on the correct pages. Even though you may teach children, remember it will be their parents and grandparents who pay the bills. All of the sites have analytics on how your ad is doing. You need to look at this weekly and see how many clicks are you getting. You may want to change some keywords, change the heading, or even increase the monthly or daily budget. The analytics will help you decide that. I personally would start with a Google Adwords for $50 a month, see what kind of results that gives you, and then adjust accordingly. I would add in the other sites after I learn and refine the process. You can run more than one ad at a time, which is a very good idea if you run more than one program. It is like having multiple business cards; it allows you to be more direct with your marketing.

Pay-per-click ads are extremely cost effective when compared to other marketing methods. Just remember to start small, actively engage yourself in your analytics, change keywords as needed, use the negative keyword option, and update the titles and descriptions as you learn what works for you. These ads are also the fastest marketing out there. Your ad will be live the same day, or maybe even the same hour. You do not have to wait like you do with printed marketing materials. Plus, pay-per-click ads allows you to conquer your niche marketing area without having to market to a mass audience.

Day 5 Challenge – Set Up a Pay-per-click Ad

- Research and choose which site to start with
- Sign up for the ad
- Set your budget
- Create the ad, keywords, negative keywords, and/or the demographics you are trying to reach
- Track your analytics and adjust accordingly

Day 6 Challenge - Email Blast

Email blast, or email marketing, is a must in today's world. There are quite a few sites out there that help you create and manage your campaign. Plus, depending on the number of email addresses you want to reach, a lot of the sites are free. A few of my favorites are: Mailchimp, Constant Contact, and Hatchback.

Emails are checked constantly thanks to the increasing presence of mobile devices. This is the fastest, most effective and cost efficient way to inform your customers, but it is not only for your active customers. Email blasts are a sales tool, too. You will want to keep every email address you ever obtain until the person unsubscribes. I like to keep a minimum of three lists - past students, current students, and prospective students. You might not send every email to all three lists, but do not forget that those past students and prospective students can become current students.

Emails are naturally action oriented. People are trained to do something with an email: reply, forward, click on a link...so give them the chance to do this. Include multiple places they can click for more information. Make sure you have the forward feature active and also make sure every email has all your social media and websites linked.

What do you send out an email about? Well, everything. Gone are the days when you sent out one email newsletter a month with all your information in it. People want short content and they want it constantly. Yes, you are going to use your email blasts to inform your customers about upcoming events or changes to a schedule, but also take the opportunity to send out your newest video on your YouTube channel, holiday greetings, lesson recaps, and awards or honors received by your business. I am not a fan of sending out purchasing emails because they annoy me as a consumer, so I cannot do it as a businessperson, either. Try for two blasts a week and see how it works for you. As with many things we have talked about in this book so far, you can create all eight email blasts for the month today and schedule them in the future.

Collecting email addresses is a must; it will take time to build up your email list, especially if you haven't already started. To build your email list, you need to make sure you are getting the email of every customer you have along with any potential customers who call or come into your business. You also need to have a link on your website for people to join your email list.

There are some guidelines to writing a great email blast. First, figure out to whom you are writing and to which list you are sending the email. You do not want to send out a class cancellation email to prospective and past customers, but you do want them to see your newest YouTube video or learn about an award your business received.

Make sure you send the right content at the right time. You do not want to send out an email asking for new students if they cannot start classes for another 4-6 weeks, just as you wouldn't wish someone Happy Thanksgiving before Halloween.

Two important facts to remember are: 1. Emails sent on the weekends have a higher opening rate than emails sent during the week. 2. Every subject line is key to opening an email. Make sure it is clear and gives a reason to read the email. Subject lines are the call to action of your email blasts.

Day 6 Challenge – Email Blast

- Find and use an email blast program
- Enter all email addresses you have and put them in the correct groups: past, current, or prospective students
- Brainstorm topics for your email blasts
- Create and schedule eight email blasts--two for every week this month

Day 7 Challenge - Knowing Your Competition

Knowing your competition is a must. By researching and keeping a watchful eye on your competition you can learn from their mistakes, model what works for them, and take things one step further than they do, which will give your business an edge on the market. The fault of so many small businesses is that they are so focused on their own business they do not even realize there is significant competition out there.

1. *You need to identify your competition.* This does not mean that if you are a music school, your only competition is other music schools. Yes, they are your direct competition, but more indirectly, so is any other activity that takes students away from your business. For example, fall soccer is a big deal in my area, as every children seems to play. Learning when the soccer season was over and advertising for those children to come join my studio really helped my growth. While the other dance studios in my area would stop taking students after September, I set up my business so that students could join classes after soccer season was done in October. This was an untapped market that I found when I started to identify my competition.

2. *What classes do they offer?* Understanding what your competitor is offering or plans to start offering can set your business apart from

45

them. Maybe you run a yoga studio and you notice that another studio does not offer parent-child classes. If you start offering them, it would set you apart from your competition. By offering different and/or special classes, you will make your business unique.

3. *Review their websites.* This is free research your competition is handing to you, so use it! Go to their websites and see what are they doing well, what seems ineffective, who owns it, who works there, what events or performances they are planning, what they charge, and what rules and policies they have. All of this information can help you to improve your business and know what areas of the market are not being reached.

4. *Follow their social media.* This is just as informational as their websites. Make sure that you check back regularly for their updates.

5. *Learn how they treat their employees.* Happy employees lead to happy students, which in turn leads to better referrals, testimonials, and more new students. How your competitors treat their employees (whether it is good or bad) is very important to know. What do they do that you can do to improve your employee relations, and what can you learn from them to never do?

Spend the day learning about your competition and how your business differs, then brainstorm changes that you can make to reach markets that are not being reached. Remember, "Keep your friends close and your enemies closer" applies to businesses, too.

Day 7 Challenge – Know Your Competition

- Identify your competition
- Understanding what they offer
- Review their websites and social media
- Learn how they treat their employees
- Set yourself apart from your competition

Day 8 Challenge - Identify Your Unique Selling Points

You spent yesterday learning all you can about your competition. Now it is time to separate yourself and make your business stand out from all the direct and indirect competition out there. You need to write your top five (or more) reasons that a potential customer should pick your business over your competition. These are known as your "Unique Selling Points" (USP), or your "Why Choose Us". USP is a clear promise to your customers of the benefits they will get with your business. The USP needs to be something your competitors cannot or do not offer. It also has to be captivating enough to attract potential students. You may have these ideas in mind already, and if you do, look at them with a skeptical eye. Now that you have done your research on your competition, ask yourself, "Are my USPs true? Are they unique? Do they make me stand out?"

Here is an example of USP for a dance studio:

- Small Class Sizes
- Age Appropriate Costumes, Music, and Movement
- Professional Dance Floors and Facility
- Lobby Area for the Whole Family
- Viewing Windows Always Open

Once you have written (or rewritten) your top 5 USP one-liners, you need to write a paragraph explaining each item in more detail. Explain why each factor is important. Answer the question, "Why, as a parent/student, do I want a business that offers these?" Now that you know your USPs, put them everywhere! Include them on your website's home page, then have a separate page that lists them with the more detailed explanations. Post one per day on social media. Make a blog post and a YouTube video on the importance of each of these points. Market these items to the point that when people call your competitors, they will ask them if their business does the same.

You can even go past five strong USPs and write 10-20. I have a checklist that I offer to email to customers who are obviously studio shopping. I would then put their email address into my database and follow up within 48 hours.

You need to teach your customers what is important in your type of business, then show them that you offer all of it. Be the educator of your customers; do not let your competition educate them for you.

Are All Dance Studios the Same?
Here is why ABC-123 School of Dance it the RIGHT Chocie!

	ABC-123	Other Dance Schools
1. Small class sizes for individualized attention.	✓	☐
2. Floating dance floor, which helps reduce the risk of injuries and allows students to dance longer without getting tired.	✓	☐
3. Full length mirrors so dancers can see their body positions while dancing.	✓	☐
4. Custom designed teaching curriculum for continual improvement and development of motor skills and dance technique.	✓	☐
5. Trained adult teaching staff.	✓	☐
6. Age appropriate costumes, music and movement.	✓	☐
7. Viewing windows always open during all regular classes.	✓	☐
8. Lobby area for the whole family. Free Wi-Fi, coffee, toy box for siblings. Families are welcome!	✓	☐
9. Dance clothes and shoes for sale for one stop shopping.	✓	☐
10. Two performance opportunities for all students; The Nutcracker and The Graduation Performance.	✓	☐
11. No hassle costumes; performance costumes are purchased, sewn and/or altered for you.	✓	☐
12. Each student receives 2 free tickets and a free cast t-shirt for each performance opportunity.	✓	☐
13. Each family receives a free DVD of each performance.	✓	☐
14. Competition teams for more performance opportunities.	✓	☐

ABC-123 School of dance 1234 Main Street, Anywhere, USA   123-456-7890   www.ABC-123dance.com

Day 8 Challenge – Identify Your Unique Selling Points

- Brainstorm why your business is unique (better than your competition)
- Write and rewrite your top 5 reasons
- Write and rewrite paragraphs for each USP explaining them in detail
- Put your USP on all your marketing materials
- Create a checklist to give out
- Create blog posts, videos, and an email blast about each USP

Day 9 Challenge - Door Hangers

Door hangers are a big bang for your buck. I have used them many times with great results. There are a lot of sites online for printing door hangers; once again my go-to site is gotprint.com. You can get 2500 of their smallest size door hangers with full color on both sides for around $130 at the time of publication.

Where to put the door hangers is key to getting good results. Start with a map of your area--a large one that you can lay out on the floor. Print out all the addresses of your current students and put a dot on the map where each family lives. You are going to find clusters of places where your students live and entire neighborhoods where no one lives. Your first instinct will be to go to the empty neighborhoods. DO NOT! There are reasons (that we may or may not know) that no one from those areas is coming to your business. It could be an area without a lot of children, too distant, economic reasons...there are so many possible factors. Instead, start with the area where most of your students come from. Once you have your large map with dots, make copies of small sections of the map. For example, if there is an average of 20 houses on a block, I would want about 25 residential blocks per map section. That way when I go out with door hangers and my map, I can hang about 500 and know exactly which areas I am targeting.

With the maps, if you have multiple groups of people going out, they will not cross paths. Or, if you are doing this over the course of a few weeks with the maps already divided up, you will not have to remember where you have already been.

Make sure you check the ordinances in the various areas you're targeting to see if door hangers are allowed. I have done this in many different towns and they all have their own rules, including everything from needing a permit to door hangers being prohibited. Just be aware and follow the guidelines. Also, do not put them in or on the mailboxes. Yes, it easier than walking up to the door in many areas, but mailboxes are strictly the property of the USPS. If you are going to put them in/on the mailboxes, you might as well be doing direct mail anyway.

When you design your door hangers, just like with everything we have talked about designing, make sure to be clear what you are offering, have a call to action, include contact information, and use pictures. Door hangers are also a great place to list your USP from yesterday's challenge.

Another option with door hangers is to team up with a local company. Door hangers have two sides, so they are pretty easy to share. You can have another company pay for the printing and you do the delivery or vice versa. I have found that insurance agents are great to pair up with. They are very willing to pay for the printing and have you deliver them. This is very helpful to them because most insurance agents do not have the staff to do this type of marketing themselves.

Door hangers do take time and effort to deliver. I have done it all: walked the areas myself, had dance team members do it as team building, and even hired people to deliver them for me. (If you are going to hire people, make sure you have a system in place for checking that they delivered them.) Although door hangers require physical exertion, do not let that scare you off; it is worth the effort.

Day 9 Challenge – Door Hangers

- Map out your current students
- Create smaller map sections of the areas you are going to target
- Look for another business to team up with
- Decide who, how, and when they will be delivered
- Design your door hangers
- Remember to check local ordinances on delivering door hangers

Day 10 Challenge - Press releases

Newspaper ads can be very pricey. Although they are effective, you probably do not have the budget to be in the newspaper year-round. However, there is free advertisement in newspapers as well. You just need to get them to write an article or even a small blurb on your business. How do you ask them to do so? Send them a press release!

Start by brainstorming ideas for a press release. It could be for new staff, new location, studio expansion, new classes, awards you or your staff have received, performances, scholarships, or one of many other options. To get your release printed in the paper, it needs to be newsworthy. If the journalist does not think it is newsworthy, it will not get printed. The best press releases are the ones that have a human interest side to them. Ask yourself the question, "How are you directly affecting the people of this community with what you have done?"

To write a press release you need to include the who, what, where, when, why, and how of the story, with the most important areas of the press release at the top. Keep it to 50 or fewer words, and use short sentences with a punch. A good press release can be printed without any additional follow-up. Make this job easy for the journalist and editors by writing a strong press release. If you have a photo, include it. If a newspaper does not have room for a full article, they may still print the photo with a caption. If this is your first time writing a press release or if you are a little nervous, check Google for one of the many examples out there for you to reference. Finally, find out how many newspapers are in your area, big or small, and send your releases to all of them.

Press Release Format

For immediate release

Title

Who, What, Where, When, Why, and How

END

For further information, please contact

Day 10 Challenge – Press Release

- o   Brainstorm topics for your press release
- o   Find contact information for all of the newspapers in your area
- o   Write your press release
- o   Email it out and remember to include a photo if you have one

Day 11 Challenge - Referrals

Today is the day you start a referral program. Referrals are your best friend. It is word-of-mouth marketing at its best. Nothing is better than a new student walking through the door because someone else sold them on your business. Remember, you cannot just expect referrals to happen--you have to ask for them. A good way to get quality referrals is not just to ask, "Who do you know?" but to ask, "Who would you like to have here in class with us?"

There are many ways to ask for a referral:

1. Directly – If you are sitting and talking with a parent, directly ask them if they know anyone who would enjoy your classes. Then give them information to pass on and tell them to bring the acquaintance to a class. You can do this with your teen students, too. They all have friends that they would like in class with them.

2. Email – Send out an email to your student base and say you are looking for referrals. Make it catchy and make them feel like quality students whose opinions you value to help bring in more quality students who can also enjoy the classes.

3. Registration – When a student registers, explain your referral program and give them information to pass on to a friend.

4.   Non-Customer – There are people who are a part of your life that love and support your business, but may not be actual customers. There is no reason they cannot bring you referrals, too.

The biggest way to get referrals is to set up a reward system. For example, offer $10 off the customer's next month's tuition for every referral brought in. Decide what you want to give away, but make it big enough to be worth it to the referrer. Then tell your customers about the program and remind them often. Just because you mentioned it once when they registered three years ago does not mean that they remember.

When you have a referral sign up, make sure you send a personal thank you note to the customer who brought in this referral. In your note, include what the "prize" is that they get for referring someone. This will make them feel like an important part of your business and will make them more likely to refer someone else. Another idea is to have a "Thank You for Your Referral" board in your waiting room. This is a great way to thank referrers, welcome newly referred students, and remind other parents about your referral program.

A different type of referral is to gain leads, also known as people's contact information. Have a contest to see who can give you the most leads. Ask for names, addresses, phone numbers, and email addresses. This is a quantity-based list--the more leads you have, the better your odds are of getting results from it. For a student contest, the one who gives you the most leads by the deadline wins. Make it something the students would want to win. Parents want free tuition, but students want gift cards, a party, cash, a popular toy, etc. Once you have these lists, get to work. Do not just let them sit there. You can send out emails, postcards, letters, or even call them (or all four!). Tell them about your business and invite them in to try a class.

Referral marketing is a strong marketing tool because of the trust factor. You trust your customers to send you new students of quality and people trust that their friends are going to send them to a good business. So much of the selling is already done because a strong level of trust has already been formed. Referrals can take time, but they have a snowball effect; once the ball gets rolling, the referrals tend to build upon each other.

Day 11 Challenge – Referral Program

- Decide what your referral program will be and what the prize(s) will be for obtaining referrals
- Start asking for referrals
- Create a contest asking for leads
- Follow up on all referrals and leads

Day 12 Challenge - Answer the Phone/Office Hours

Did you know that more than half of the callers sent to voicemail do not leave a message? Nowadays nobody wants to leave a message and wait for you to call back. Please answer your phone! You would think this would be obvious and not need a day in our marketing challenge, but you would be amazed at the number of business that do not answer their phones.

Running businesses that have classes mostly in the evening can be challenging because we do not have the normal 9-5 office hours. Additionally, our instant gratification-craving society makes many people think your business should be open 24 hours. I am not suggesting you do that, but you do need to have office hours. Keep the office hours simple and consistent. Closing 30 minutes differently everyday is just frustrating to people. Plus, having office hours when no one is there to help is just as frustrating. Make sure you have someone in the office to answer the phone and great people who come in. This is the first face and voice of your business; I do not suggest just grabbing anyone. This needs to be a professional person with a good rapport and knowledge of your business.

I cannot stress enough the importance of answering the phone. When you do not answer the phone a lot happens. You may lose a prospect, or you could aggravate an already aggravated customer. By not answering your phone you cannot answer questions or solve problems. Also (and this is the biggest issue), not answering the phone is throwing time, effort, and money out the window. This is day 10 of the 30-day marketing challenge, and everything we have done is to bring in new students to your business; however, if you are not answering the phone, those new students will go somewhere else.

This is not just about answering the phone, but also about answering it professionally. Always answer the phone with a smile–you can hear a smile! Answer the phone quickly–preferably before the third ring. Mention your business's name when answering the phone so that callers know they've reached the right place. Mention your first name to start a personal bond with the caller. Do not multitask while on the phone, because it is obvious and rude. Give the caller your complete attention.

Make sure that the staff members who answer the phone can answer the questions that come in. They should be able to register students and be familiar with pricing, classes, policies. Writing out a phone script of the most common types of phone calls is helpful for office staff. I am not sure which is more annoying--having my phone call go to voicemail or having it answered by a person who is unable to help me. If a message has to be taken because you cannot answer their question, 1. Make sure you read the caller's contact info back to them to insure you have it correct, and 2. Give them a time frame in which you will be able to return the call with an appropriate answer.

Now we all know we cannot answer the phone 24 hours a day. Make sure your voicemail message is clear. I like to add to the outgoing message that we are always open online, then give our web address. Finally, return the messages ASAP. Just remember that every phone call you do not answer becomes a sale opportunity for your competitor.

Day 12 Challenge – Answer the Phone/Office Hours

- Create office hours and have someone present to answer the phone
- Create a pleasant outgoing voicemail message that informs the caller when you will return their call
- Write a phone script and review it with any and all people who will answer the phone
- Answer the phone and convert every caller into a new student

Day 13 Challenge - Letters to Teachers

Children spend an average of 40 hours a week with their teachers at school; add in extra curricular activities and that number becomes much larger than a full-time work week. In many cases they are spending more time with their schoolteachers than their own parents.

Teachers are a great connection between you and new students. Start building relationships with the teachers in your area and they will start sending students your way. I would start off with a letter to all the teachers who work with children who you think would benefit from your school. For example, if you are a music school, make sure the band and orchestra teachers know about your classes.

Research all the schools in your area and find the teachers who not only teach classes that are a good fit for your business, but also work with the students of after-school activities that could benefit from your expertise, too. I would include school counselors, resource teachers, and the full group of elementary school teachers. Parents are always asking teachers for advice, so it would be nice if the teachers suggested your business.

A few tips on writing the letter: even if you type the letter, I still suggest handwriting the address on the envelope. Studies show that a handwritten envelope is almost three times more likely to be opened. Introduce yourself and your business, then explain how your business could benefit their students. Keep it short and sweet, and try not to be too formal. You want the letter to sound like a personal letter, not a sales pitch. I would throw in a few business cards, and if your business is having an upcoming performance or event, I would send them two free tickets. This is a very simple way to get you name out to another person who can help promote your business.

Day 13 Challenge – Letters to Teachers

- o Gather names of teachers
- o Write letters
- o Mail the letters with a few business cards and even some tickets to an upcoming performance or event

Day 14 Challenge - Sell to Current Students

When you want to increase enrollment, you either have to get more students or sell more to the students you have. This is true with any business. Today we are going to spend the day selling to your current student base. Let us talk numbers (theses are nice round numbers that make math easy, not a suggestion of pricing for your business.) Let us say you have 100 students who all take one class a month at $50 a month for 10 months. In one year, you have $50,000. You could really add another 25 students without having to add classes or pay your teachers more. You send out an email (which is free) to your current student base to take a second class for half price. 25 students take you up on this deal. You have now gained $6,250 a year without spending anything on marketing, adding any classes, or paying more staff. That is $6,250 a year of straight profit. Not too bad! Let us brainstorm some ways to sell to your current students:

Invite current students to take a second class and offer a discount. Send out an email to your student base, but before you do, figure out what kind of discount you want to have. Also figure out what classes have room--you might have to be selective with who you make the offer to. You do not want to invite everyone when you only have room in your preschool classes, for example.

Schedule certain classes back-to-back to encourage students to enroll in more than one class. When you are working on your scheduling, remember that parents are more likely to sign up for a second class if it does not mean another day of travel.

Add an extra 30 minutes onto various classes to work on a specific skill. This is a great, simple strategy. For example, if you are a gymnastics school and you have a group of students who really want to learn a back handspring, why not offer an optional 30 minutes of back handspring work after their normal class? You can also add clinics that meet two, three, or four times for a one-time fee to work on specific skills.

Start a new comparable program. If you teach dance, why not add in music or tumbling? This is a bigger undertaking than just adding in a class here or there, but it is a great way to grow your business. You can also find a new program that will sell well to siblings or parents, or even a business that needs to rent space to use during hours you are not normally open.

Start a performance group that attends a specific class. My favorite example of doing this at my dance studio was offering a one-hour class for anyone who wanted to be in the opening production number of our spring recital. I would announce it in March and practice up until recital. It was a great way to make some extra money toward the end of our season, and the children loved being part of this special group. What can you come up with?

No matter if you pick a 30-minute add on class or start a completely new program, selling to your current students will guarantee that you bring in more revenue and even more new students.

Day 14 Challenge – Sell to Current Students

- o Figure out which ways you are going to sell more to your current students
- o Put your plan into action!

Day 15 Challenge - Call Past Students

Today you get on the phone and call past students. Children change activities frequently for various reasons, and luckily, more often than not, the reason is not you. Just because they did not sign up last session does not mean they will not come back and sign up this session. Get on the phone and call them!

First, gather a list of all your past students and figure out some information about them. You may know that a particular student moved or graduated, and you probably have one or two students who you would not want back anyway for the difficulties they caused. Go through your list and cross off those students. Then, write down for the rest of the list: how old they are now, which class(es) they took before, and notes on any significant things you remember about them. This could be anything--a funny story, another activity they loved, or the name of a sibling. You just want something that can help make your phone call sound personal. Next, figure out which classes would be a good fit for them now and why. You do not want to call and talk someone into coming back to your business, then realize that you have no place to put them.

Now make a goal. It can be something like, "I will call 50 families today and every day until I have called them all," or, "I will call till I get three students signed up." A goal will keep you on track and help make today's challenge seem doable.

One more thing before you start calling--write a script, or two, or three. The phone calls will go much smoother with a script. When you are trying to sell to someone, you want to get them to say yes three times during the phone call, and a script can help you do that.

Sample Script:

Hello, Carla, this is Beth from ABC Judo. How is your Friday going?

We miss your son, Alex, and I wanted to tell you there is a new Friday class for his age level. Would he like to come for a free trial?

If the answer is yes, confirm a date and time, then close with, "We will see you Friday!"

If the answer is maybe or, "I'll ask him," close with, "Okay, if he is interested we would really like to see him. Just drop in at 5 p.m. on Friday, or we can set a time that is good for you." (Pause to let them say if another time works best, and if they have another choice, schedule them for that day). "We have a class at 6 p.m. on Tuesday; I'll schedule him as a guest that day. Thanks, and have a good day!"

If the answer is no, say, "We enjoyed having him in class and would like to have students as nice (or smart, interesting, or attentive) as your son. Please recommend us to your friends. Thanks for your time!"

Day 15 Challenge – Call Past Students

- Collect the names and numbers of past students
- Make notes on age, classes, and personal interests of each student
- Set a goal
- Write your scripts
- Start calling!

Day 16 Challenge - Free Clinics/Classes

Free, Free, Free! – everyone loves free. A lot of you reading this probably already do free trial classes or have free clinics. The problem is not in the offering of the free class, but in the follow-through after the students have left.

Before I get into the follow-through let us quickly discuss what free classes you can offer. First, I let anyone have a free trial class. This just eases the worry parents may have about signing their children up in a class and having them not like it. Generally, nine out of ten times they sign up for the class afterwards. If you have hired a new teacher or you are starting a new class, a free trial class is a great way to spark interest with your current student base. Also, offer free clinics to groups outside of your business. Preschools, scout groups, clubs, and school organizations are just a handful of the many options to pick from.

Once you have a plan for free classes and clinics, you need to have a form for them to sign before starting the class. Name, address, phone number, email, age, and a liability waiver (if needed). This form is a must because this is where the follow-through happens. Now that you have the form with all of the customer's information, you can add them to your email list of prospective students. This is another great way to build up your list for your email blasts. Just because they do not sign up today, this month, or even this year does not mean that they will not keep up to date with your business and possibly join in the future. Send them a thank you card or a postcard in the mail. Children love to get mail, and this is so simple to do. Then a week or so later, if they haven't come back, call them. Tell them you enjoyed having them at your business and invite them to join a class. This is such a simple process that if you have procedures in place, the follow-through of your free trials and clinics will not take up much time.

Also, you need to send the children home with information. For example, you have a free clinic for a scout group. There are ten students who come in two vans; most of the parents do not come with them. Send them home with information on your business and invite them back for a free trial class. Then when they go home and tell their parents how much fun they had and that they want to take classes, the parents have information to review about your business.

Day 16 Challenge – Free Trial Classes and Clinics

- If you do not already do so, start offering free trial classes
- Develop your registration form for free trials and clinics
- Plan your follow-up procedures
- Plan two or three free clinics for preschools, scout groups, clubs, or school organizations in the area
- Remember to follow up with each student

Day 17 Challenge - Postcards

I love postcards as much as I love business cards. You can use them for so many things, and plus, children love to get mail.

For starters, I always send a happy birthday postcard to every student on his or her birthday, even the adult students. It is just a nice way to let them know you are thinking about them. I also send a postcard to any student who misses two classes in a row. I have found that if a student misses three classes in a row without any contact, they are most likely not going to come back. Sending them a postcard that lets them know you miss them is a great way to keep in contact with them. I send welcome postcards to everyone who registers, and I write what classes they will be taking and when their first class will be.

87

Thank you postcards are another type that I use. You can never go wrong with sending someone a thank you note. I make sure to send a thank you postcard after any free trials or clinics. Postcards are also nice for reaching out to all those students you called that have not signed up for classes yet. My favorite use for postcards is a "good job" note. Having your teachers send out one or two postcards a week telling a student or two that they are doing a great job in class builds confidence and loyalty much more than you would imagine.

There are so many uses for postcards, and for the price, you can't beat the value. Deciding when and why you are going to send postcards and having the postcards already made up makes this much easier to follow through on sending them.

Day 17 Challenge – Postcards

- o Decide when and why you will be using postcards
- o Design and order the appropriate cards
- o Start sending them out!

Day 18 Challenge - Community Outreach

Community outreach is about giving back to your community and getting your name visible in your community. There is so much you can do in your area. Performances, parades, volunteer work, donations, etc., all work toward the goal of giving, but that does not mean you will not end up getting students from those activities if you do them well and do them often. Today, take sometime and think of what you, as a business, can do for your community.

I am a strong believer in contributing to any local raffle, auction, or donation for a good cause. If any organization comes and asks for an auction donation, give them one. It is easy advertisement. You can do anything from one month to a full year of free classes, or even one special event, like a camp or clinic. Decide what you want to give, then design and print some certificates now. That way, when anyone comes in and asks for a donation, you have your certificates ready to hand out right away. Yes, it can cost you money to give away a free month (or more) of classes, but think about what you are gaining. A new student (who will likely continue to take classes), name recognition, and advertisement through the organization that is hosting the event. That said, this opportunity is well worth some free class time. Do remember to put an expiration date on these certificates or they could show up years later. Do not wait for someone to ask, either; if you know of an event coming up, go ahead and offer your donation.

Performances, parades, and community events are great for your business and your students. This category does not include participation in competitions or your business's yearly performances. Rather, I am talking about giving free performances in your community. Maybe your town has a festival or fair in which you can perform. Dance studios should get involved in National Dance Week and gyms should promote National Gymnastics Day. There is likely a national week or day for anything you teach. If not, start one! A performance gets your name out and shows the general public what you offer at your business. It is also a great sales pitch for incoming students because you are giving them the opportunity to perform.

Another thing to remember is that you cannot just perform, then walk away. You need to have yourself, staff, and/or even trusted parents working the crowd. Hand out business cards, flyers, or even balloons (all children love balloons) with your business's name on them.

Never forget the power of volunteer work. Volunteering encourages teamwork, creates a positive atmosphere, and improves communication between staff, students, and parents who participate. It will also enhance your business's reputation, brand awareness, and loyalty among customers. Additionally, it just feels good to take a step away from daily life and spend a day volunteering. People like to support businesses that support a cause.

Always wear your business's t-shirts when you do any community outreach, and remember that all community outreach can make for a good press release and/or YouTube videos.

Day 18 Challenge – Community Outreach

- o Decide what your regular donations will be and create a few certificates to give out throughout the year to area auctions
- o Plan a performance in your community
- o Find a cause or organization to team up with and have a volunteering event for your business
- o Brainstorm other ways you can have your business play an active role in your community

Day 19 Challenge - Meet-ups/Deal Sites

Meet-ups are where people of similar interests organize offline events. It takes social media and makes it a face-to-face experience. You can use meet-ups to help market your business, but remember that people who attend meets-ups do not want to be sold to, they want to learn and socialize. If meet-ups are a new concept to you, spend some time today learning about them online.

Start a meet-up group based on an interest related to your business. You can charge a small fee to offset the costs of the meet-up if you need, but this is not a moneymaking area. Rather, it is a way to spark interest, get people into your business, and have them market for you through word-of-mouth. The key to choosing a good meet-up topic is to pick something narrow and unique. Think carefully about how you can relate your meet-up to what you teach, because the goal is to feed these people (or their kids) into your business.

Meet-up Ideas:
- Dancing with your baby for exercise; then, once a participant's baby is two years old, they can go into a "mommy and me" class. You can do the same with gymnastics, martial arts, music, etc.

- Toddler play-date
- Moms walking with strollers--meet at your business and go for a walk

Once you have decided what your meet-ups will be about, start holding regular meet-up events sponsored by your business. They can be informal groups, workshops, seminars, or just a group that gets together over coffee for topic-based discussions.

This creates a social network, and you should use it to socialize yourself. Join similar meet-ups hosted by others--hang out, interact with them, and focus on forming networking relationships. There are various sites you can use to find these groups, such as Meetup.com and Citysocializer.com, but you can also find and create your meet-ups through social media groups on Facebook, Twitter, and LinkedIn.

Online deal sites, such as groupon.com and livingsocial.com, provide another beneficial marketing tool. Theses sites are great for short-term clinics, camps, or even new classes you may be offering. They are a way to get potential clients in the door and try out your business. Once they walk through your doors, though, it is your job to sell to them and keep them as customers after using the deal they purchased. Follow-up is key!

Day 19 Challenge – Meet-ups/Deal Sites

- Create a meet-up group and schedule events
- Create a deal though deal sites

Day 20 Challenge - Testimonials

If you are not collecting and using testimonials, you are missing out on a great sales tool. Testimonials build trust and help potential customers overcome skepticism. A good testimonial has the ability to convince even your toughest sell that your business is right for them.

One easy way to collect testimonials is to include a page on your website with a form that your customers can use to give their feedback, such as, "Click here to let us know what you think!" Put this link next to some testimonials that you have already gathered to give customers an example of the kind of feedback you seek. Anytime you receive a great email from a customer, ask if you can use their comments as a testimonial. Since they are already pleased with your services, they will most likely be thrilled to help show support for your business. Remember, you can also use Survey Monkey or Facebook to set up a poll that asks for feedback related to your business in order to acquire testimonials.

Include your best testimonials front and center on your website's homepage and wherever possible on all other pages. This way, no matter what page your visitors see, they will find a positive customer review of your business. Also, set up a separate page for all your superior testimonials.

Post testimonials on your social media pages. You can even tag the person who gave you the testimonial so their friends see it, too. You can place a testimonial at the end of each blog post and email blast as a signature line. Put testimonials in your printed material and even hang them up in your business for other customers to see.

Video testimonials are even better than written ones because of the personal connection you feel when you see a person giving the testimonial. Take a video camera or even just your phone to your next large event, and ask various customers if they would give a quick 3-5 sentence testimonial on your business. These can be shared everywhere, too.

Day 20 Challenge - Testimonials

- o Start collecting testimonials
- o Send out surveys and polls asking for feedback
- o Set up a form on your website to collect testimonials
- o Ask specific customers to write one for you
- o Ask customers to share testimonials on video
- o Post testimonials to your website, social media, blogs, in your email blasts, and on printed materials

Day 21 Challenge - Direct Mail

According to the United States Postal Service, 98 percent of people retrieve their mail daily, and 77 percent of people sort it immediately. Direct Mail is not dead; it is the only medium with which you can reach every household in your community. Even better than that, you can choose who you specifically want to reach. You can pick your demographics, such as households with children in a certain age range within a certain income range. When picking areas to send your postcards, go back to the maps we made during Challenge Day #9 and see which are your strongest areas. Direct mail is very targeted marketing.

Many of us have the idea that direct mail is expensive, but it is not anymore. USPS offers a service called "Every Door Direct Mail"-- just look it up on their website. For example, if I order 5,000 full color, 5"x7" postcards from gotprint.com for about $200, I can mail these through USPS's "Every Door Direct Mail" service for around $800 in my area. That comes to about $0.20 each, including printing and postage. This is less than the cost of a postcard stamp, which is currently $0.34. Now I have spent $1,000 on this direct marketing campaign. With my example of a student taking one class at $50 a month and staying an average of two years, I only need one new student to sign up from this campaign to pay for it. This makes it seem much more affordable!

The design of your postcard has just as must impact as to whom you send them. As with everything else we have talked about designing in this 30-day challenge, you need a clear call to action, a picture that fits what you are selling, and easily identifiable contact information. If graphic design is not your strong point, you could find a graphic design student to whip one up for you for $50. There are also full-service companies who will do it all for you. It just depends on your willingness to do the extra work to find one along with your budget for this campaign to determine which is a better route for you to take.

Day 21 Challenge – Direct Mail

- Research the USPS service called "Every Door Direct Mail" along with other companies who offer direct mail
- Pick your areas to target
- Design your postcard
- Decide on your budget
- Mail!

Day 22 Challenge - Banners/Signs/Yard Signs

You need to make your business visible in as many places as you can. Banners, signs, yard signs, and car magnets will help with your visibility. You may think, "I've been here for 30 years--everyone knows where I am." On the contrary, people just do not pay that much attention to their surroundings. Plus, the average American moves 11.7 times in his or her life, so there are always new families in your area.

To start today's challenge, walk outside your business and look at it. Do you have a sign? Is it in good shape? Can you see it when walking by? When driving by? Does the sign indicate what you do? Does your business center have a marquee and are you on it? If you answered no to any of these questions, it is time to get to work.

Once you have done that, let us talk about additional signage you can use. Temporary signage is good because it changes the scenery and makes someone who may drive by everyday notice that something is different. My favorite signs are large, full-color banners. I would display two of these in front of my studio during peak registration times. They included a great photo and a call to action. They're simple to order, and because of advances in digital printing, they are affordable. You should be able to get a 5'x7' full-color banner for around $100. Make sure your banners are always mounted nicely without sagging or loose ends that will flap in the wind. Do not leave your banners up year-round; the point is to change the scenery.

Another option to try is a clapboard sign on your walkway. This is an especially good idea if you are in a more high-traffic area.

Yard signs are a good way to get visible advertisement in neighborhoods. You can get 100 full-color, double-sided signs for around $150. Hand these to students and have them put them in their yards. You can give one to anyone who registers, or limit it to students who make it into a special performance group, team, or level--anything will work. Also, depending on where you live, you can put signs on the corner of busy intersections. Just make sure they are clear and easy to read with a website, phone number, and call to action. Most people will only have a few moments to read a yard sign, so large letters and short, clear phrases will make the information easier to absorb.

Car magnets are another inexpensive but effective advertising tool. They can allow you to turn your car into a moving billboard. Just like with yard signs, people will only have a few moments to read the magnet, so be clear and concise.

Day 22 Challenge – Banners/Signs/Yard Signs

- Do an outside sign assessment of your business and fix any problems
- Design and order full color banners
- Design and order yard signs
- Design and order car magnets

Day 23 Challenge - Person-to-Person Marketing

Person-to-person marketing (a.k.a. approaching people) is your best marketing tool. No one loves your business more than you. No one knows more about your business than you. No one can sell your business better than you. Do not be afraid to approach people. There are always energetic children dancing down the aisle of a grocery store, or kids doing flips on the monkey bars of a playground. How about the one child who sings constantly or that child who can drum a beat anywhere--we have all seen them. Now invite them to your business. It does not take much--just walk up to their parent with two business cards and say, "Looks like your little boy loves music. You should sign him up for a class." Then smile and walk away. Parents want to hear how sweet, wonderful, and talented their children are, so be the person who tells them that.

Approaching people is not just about the crazy kid and tired parent you see on the playground. Everyone knows someone who has a kid. This is when you need your elevator pitch. What is an elevator pitch, you might ask? It is a few seconds to leave an exciting and meaningful impression about your business on anyone with whom you come in contact. The best elevator pitches leave the other person with a question, which can then lead to a longer conversation about your business.

There are a few tips to remember when writing your elevator pitch. This is not a 60-second advertisement during which only you speak and then walk away; your goal is to have a two-way conversation. A successful pitch makes the other person smile and say, "Interesting. Tell me more." Keep it short--think 10 seconds, not 60! And please use everyday language and one-syllable words. Start with an intriguing or puzzling answer to the question, "What do you do?" Then explain exactly what you do after prompting the person to ask, "How?" or stare at you in a confused manner. Last, shift into a story, create a mental picture, or give an example of what you do so they can clearly see it.

Elevator pitch example for a gymnastics business:
What do you do?
I burn energy off of children.
Huh?

I own ABC gymnastics school, where not only do we tire out your children with fun-filled gymnastics classes, but we also train them to do the skills correctly.

Be ready to approach people, know your elevator pitch, keep your eyes out for potential customers, and have your business cards ready.

Day 23 Challenge – Approach People

- Write (and probably rewrite) your elevator pitch
- Practice it a lot!
- Make sure you always have business cards on hand
- Go out and approach people
- Encourage teachers and staff to do the same

Day 24 Challenge - T-shirts

T-shirts are a great marketing tool, and if done right, they will get used and not tossed. T-shirts turn your students into walking billboards. When creating t-shirts, you want a fun simple design that stands out and fits with your business's image and mission. T-shirts create strong brand recognition, so the more people that wear them, the more eyes will see and learn about your business.

Do not always charge for your t-shirts. You are not in the apparel business (I assume), so do not always try to make t-shirts be a profitable part of your business. They are advertising, and there is no need to make people pay to advertise your business for you. T-shirt companies are all over the country, and the costs of shirts have significantly decreased because of their widespread availability, so shop around.

There are many ways to get your t-shirts out in public. The easiest way is to make a new design every year and give one to every child who registers. You can also give them out to students who do a free trial class or people who attend your meet-ups. You could host a social media contest and the winner would get a free t-shirt. Give away t-shirts as thank you gifts to your best customers, or to your student of the month. Also, give them to friends and staff who you know will wear them. Finally, always remember to wear them yourself. When people ask you about your shirt, you can give them your elevator pitch from Challenge Day #23 and hand them a few business cards.

When designing your t-shirt, remember to be bold, be creative, and be inspiring. Yes, that is a lot to expect out of a t-shirt, but it is not just a t-shirt--this is marketing for your business.

Day 24 Challenge – T-shirts

- o Come up with a new t-shirt design
- o Decide who you will give them to and who is going to order them
- o Find the best price available for printing (not compromising quality)
- o Order them and start wearing your t-shirts

Day 25 Challenge - Online Reviews

Online reviews are the lifeline of your online marketing. Having a great Search Engine Optimization (SEO), website, and social media presence will do you no good if you have limited or negative online reviews. Nine out of ten consumers read online reviews for local businesses. Online reviews make your business more trustworthy, because most people trust online reviews as much as a personal recommendation. Remember, though, that this trust is dependent on the authenticity of the review. If you have two equivalent businesses and one has better online reviews while the other ignores the importance of reviews, the first one will definitely have better traffic to their site. This makes for a better conversion rate into students. Here is a list of popular review sites:

- Amazon
- Angie's List
- Better Business Bureau (BBB)
- Bing Places
- Citysearch
- Consumer Reports
- Demand Force (newer review site)
- Dex Knows

- DoneRight.com
- Epinions.com
- Google+ Local/Google Places
- Insider Pages
- Judy's Book
- MerchantCircle
- Yahoo! Local
- Yellow Pages
- Yelp!
- LinkedIn
- Facebook

They may not all be relevant to your business; however, many industry specific associations, organizations, and directories offer reviews on their sites, which are not listed here.

Spend the day looking to see where you have reviews and how good your ratings are. If you have bad reviews you can either respond or ignore, but do not get emotional about them. I find the best response to be, "I am sorry you were not happy with your experience, and we would like to fix it. Please give us a call at 123-345-6789."

Now, you need to seek out some good (or great) reviews! The best way is to ask. I would not send out a blanket email blast to everyone asking for reviews; rather, I would pick specific customers who you know will write good reviews. Make it easy and simple for them--be specific with what you would like. Do not tell them to just go to any site and write a review. Give them a specific site and step-by-step directions on how to post the review. The easier you make it, the more willing people will be to do this for you.

Day 25 Challenge - Online Reviews

- o Search the various online review sites and see how you are doing
- o Ask specific people to write reviews for you

Day 26 Challenge - Networking Groups

Even in our social, online society, face-to-face networking groups provide a key to good business. People will always do business with people they know, long before they will do business with people they find through advertising. Networking is not about making direct sales--it is about getting professional connections and extremely valuable word-of-mouth advertising.

There are some key ways to get networking groups to work for you. First, find a networking group that compliments you and your business. You will want a group in which you can become memorable to the other members. Whether you choose a networking group of similar businesses or a group involved in philanthropy that is near to your heart, you will want to find a group or groups that fit you as a both a business and as a person.

Second, the only way anyone is going to remember who you are and what you do is if you show up regularly. Make your attendance a priority. The reward of networking does not happen overnight. You will need to devote a few months or more for it to really take effect, but it can pay off immensely.

You are not only networking for new students, but you are also networking for business relations. Through your networking groups, you may find a business to team-up with you on door hangers (Challenge Day 9) or a business with whom you can do promotion (Challenge Day 28). Additionally, you may find businesses that can give you price breaks on items you use for your business. Say you meet someone who does digital printing--they might be willing to give you a better price on all of your advertisements. Maybe you meet a banker (or several--they love networking groups!), and he or she can give you a better rate on credit card processing. Who knows, you might even meet a landlord who can lower your rent! Sometimes networking is not about gaining a student, but about cutting costs that can allow you to then grow your bottom line. In revisiting my example of one student bringing you a $1,000 a year, if you end up cutting $3,000 in costs through networking, that is no different than gaining three new students.

Day 26 Challenge – Networking Groups

- Find one or two networking groups to join
- Attend the meetings regularly
- Start building strong personal and professional relationships

Day 27 Challenge - Blogs

A blog can be a powerful marketing tool for your business. A good blog will make you the authority figure within your area of business. You can post content that is helpful to your readership and provide an effective way to not only entertain, but also to educate your readers. Blogs create opportunities for sharing via social media sites, which in turn gives you free advertisement. Blogs help grow your email list and can turn consumers into students.

Today it is time to start, or refine, your blog. A good blog has a clear topic with your own personality added in throughout. To make yourself an authority figure in the eyes of your readers, you need to refine your topic. A blog is not the place to be a jack-of-all-trades. What topics do you have a lot to say about?--start there. A blog post should be about 100-400 words. If you have more than 400 words to say about a topic, look at how you can turn them into two or more posts.

Blogs also need a call to action, and/or something that makes the readers comment, share, and want to read the next blog. You can start an active conversation with your blog, but if you close off the conversation with inactivity or dull content, it will not be effective.

A good blogger posts many times during a week. Although this can take a long time, you could write several posts in one day, then schedule them to post throughout the month. You do not need to sit at your computer each day to write a blog post. Once you get your topic refined, you can knock out 10-20 in one sitting.

Lastly, when writing your blog and blog title, do not forget your SEO keywords. Also, make sure your social media sites are linked to your blog, as well as your website. All of these areas work together to give you top placement on search engines, which then leads to more visibility and more students. Remember, you have to share your blog yourself--you cannot expect people to find it. Tell them about it through email, social media, and word-of-mouth.

Note: This chapter is 363 words.

Day 27 Challenge – Blogs

- o Sign up for a blog page
- o Figure out your refined topic
- o Brainstorm post ideas
- o Start writing
- o Post and share

Day 28 Challenge - Promote with Other Businesses

Teaming up with other businesses can really boost your numbers. There are a lot of ways to do this. The simplest one is to ask other stores in your plaza or strip mall if you can put flyers on their counters, and then let them do the same. It is always nice to build good rapport with your neighbors. Then, when one of their customers asks about your business, they will have good things to say.

Team up with a business that relates to your business. If you teach music, team up with an instrument shop so that each of you can send clients to the other's business. The same can go for dance studios and dance supply stores. When it comes to any supplies that your students might need for their classes, if you do not sell them, you need to form a partnership with the businesses that do. Another type of business you can team up with is one that is indirectly related to your business. For example, gymnasts need dance lessons to perfect their competitive routines. You can also team up with a business who can use your space during your non-peak hours.

No matter how you promote with other businesses, just remember that we are all in the market together. It never hurts to help out another business; it could help your business, too.

Day 28 Challenge – Promote with Other Businesses

- Meet all the businesses in your shopping center, and ask if you can swap out advertising at each other's businesses
- Team up with businesses that sell items your students may need
- Find a business that could use your space during non-peak hours

Day 29 Challenge - Information in Windows/Outdoor Fliers

Information in your windows and outdoor fliers are a must, especially if your business does not have the staff to have 9 a.m. to 9 p.m. office hours. Whether people come to you business on purpose or they just happened to see it and stop by, people will always be walking by when you are closed and want to see some information. Why lose potential new students over something as simple as this?

Start with a full-color flier in your front window. Say what classes you offer, to what age groups, and if and when you are accepting new students. This is a good place to highlight awards, certifications, and/or education your staff has, plus, your windows are a nice place to highlight any upcoming clinics, performances, or events. Always make sure your information is current; you do not want a flyer from 6 months ago with last year's classes still posted. This looks unprofessional and can make it appear that your business is no longer running, especially when you are already closed for the day and the lights are out.

For the outdoor fliers, you might not want to do full-color because it can get pricey, but you will at least want a nice informational piece that has similar information to what is in the window, along with a call to action, contact information, office hours, and your website.

You will need to trade out the fliers every once in awhile. They will start to look dirty and weathered, and that is not the image you want to project of your business. I put out three to five at a time and replace them weekly (or sooner if the box is empty).

This is a small item that will make a big impact on your business, so try not to let it slip through the cracks. I find that we all have that one very helpful student; this is a great task to ask him or her to help with. Once you have the information created, ask the student to make sure new, fresh fliers are always outside and to take down any information from the windows that is no longer current. Trust me, the student will love it!

Day 29 Challenge – Information in Windows/Outdoor Fliers
- Create information to place in your windows
- Create fliers to put outside your business
- Ask a student to help keep the information looking fresh and up to date

Day 30 Challenge - CLEAN!

Depending on your personality, you are either going to love or hate today's challenge, but either way it has to be done. We all go blind to the way a business looks when we spend so much time there, and if you are working with children, it is pretty hard to keep up with the messes they make. The cleanliness of your space is the first impression people will get when they come into your business, so you want it to be a good one. I am always skeptical of businesses that are not well kept, especially if they are working with my children. If they do not have good upkeep in regards to cleanliness and presentation, it makes me think they will not pay good enough attention to my children.

Have someone who can be honest and unbiased tell you your business's cleaning (or repair) needs. Let someone who does not spend a lot of time at your business look for these things, because when you spend a lot of time in a place, you can go blind to all the things around you that need attention. Have the person start outside from a parking spot, just like a potential student would. Look around the parking lot, the walkway, and the front door. Then have your helper walk through the business and point out everything he or she sees that needs cleaning or work. Follow along so that you can see the issues as your potential patron would.

This is not just about physical cleanliness; it is also about the staging of the business. It might be time to replace the area rug in your waiting room. Maybe you have very outdated pictures (or none at all) hanging up in your lobby that need replacing. Maybe your business smells--I know a lot of gyms and dance studios do. A plant in the lobby can help significantly with smells. Maybe you just have too much clutter. A fresh coat of paint can go a long way! If you have a group of teenagers, they can get that done for you in an afternoon, and it will only cost you the price of the paint and a few pizzas. You want to emit a calming and inviting environment.

A clean business is not only good for potential students, but it also creates a pleasant work environment for your employees. It makes them realize that the business is important to you, and they will model your attitude. This also does the same for your current clients. If they see you cleaning, fixing, and updating your business, they will recognize that you care about the appearance of your business and that you plan to keep it going for years to come. A clean business shows respect!

Day 30 Challenge – CLEAN!

- o Ask someone to do a cleanliness assessment on your business
- o Listen to their suggestions and clean!

REPEAT!

Congratulations are in order. You just successfully made it through this 30-day marketing challenge. The big question is how many students have you gained. Let us find out.

# of students	−	# of students	=	# of students gained
enrolled today		on page 13		from 30-day challenge

No matter what your number is, you have grown because of this challenge. You now have a bigger and better understanding of marketing along with a better understanding of your business's "Unique Selling Points," or USP.

This book is not a one-time deal; you need to repeat it-- monthly. Marketing is a continuous process and soon it will be second nature to you. Each time you repeat the steps in this book, you will grow in numbers as well as in your knowledge of business marketing.

Before you go back to the beginning, let us take a few minutes to assess what you have done by answering the following questions:

1. Which day did I earn the most students?
2. Which day did I earn the least (or no) students?

3. Which day was the hardest and why?

4. Which day was the easiest and why?

5. Which day did I not try my best?

Now you get to REPEAT!

Made in the USA
San Bernardino, CA
19 July 2017